THIS PLANNER BELONGS TO

_____

_____

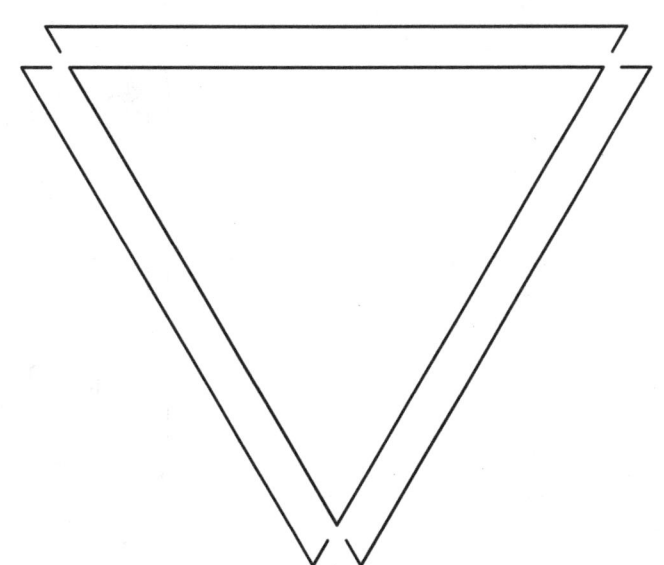

TWITTER POSTS *PLANNER*

POST

_____
_____
_____
_____

POST NUMBER _____

POST DATE _____

NOTES _____
_____

POST

_____
_____
_____
_____

POST NUMBER _____

POST DATE _____

NOTES _____
_____

POST

_____
_____
_____
_____

POST NUMBER _____

POST DATE _____

NOTES _____
_____

TWITTER POSTS *PLANNER*

POST

_____
_____
_____
_____

POST NUMBER _____

POST DATE _____

NOTES _____
_____

POST

_____
_____
_____
_____

POST NUMBER _____

POST DATE _____

NOTES _____
_____

POST

_____
_____
_____
_____

POST NUMBER _____

POST DATE _____

NOTES _____
_____

TWITTER POSTS *PLANNER*

POST

_____

_____

_____

_____

POST NUMBER _____

POST DATE _____

NOTES _____

_____

POST

_____

_____

_____

_____

_____

POST NUMBER _____

POST DATE _____

NOTES _____

_____

POST

_____

_____

_____

_____

POST NUMBER _____

POST DATE _____

NOTES _____

_____

TWITTER POSTS *PLANNER*

POST

_____
_____
_____
_____

POST NUMBER _____

POST DATE _____

NOTES _____
_____

POST

_____
_____
_____
_____

POST NUMBER _____

POST DATE _____

NOTES _____
_____

POST

_____
_____
_____
_____

POST NUMBER _____

POST DATE _____

NOTES _____
_____

TWITTER POSTS *PLANNER*

POST

_____

_____

_____

_____

_____

| POST NUMBER _____ |
| POST DATE _____ |
| NOTES _____
 _____ |

POST

_____

_____

_____

_____

_____

| POST NUMBER _____ |
| POST DATE _____ |
| NOTES _____
 _____ |

POST

_____

_____

_____

_____

_____

| POST NUMBER _____ |
| POST DATE _____ |
| NOTES _____
 _____ |

TWITTER POSTS *PLANNER*

POST

_____
_____
_____
_____

POST NUMBER _____

POST DATE _____

NOTES _____
_____

POST

_____
_____
_____
_____

POST NUMBER _____

POST DATE _____

NOTES _____
_____

POST

_____
_____
_____
_____

POST NUMBER _____

POST DATE _____

NOTES _____
_____

TWITTER POSTS *PLANNER*

POST

_____

POST NUMBER	_____
POST DATE	_____
NOTES	_____

POST

_____

POST NUMBER	_____
POST DATE	_____
NOTES	_____

POST

_____

POST NUMBER	_____
POST DATE	_____
NOTES	_____

TWITTER POSTS *PLANNER*

POST

_____
_____
_____
_____

POST NUMBER _____

POST DATE _____

NOTES _____
_____

POST

_____
_____
_____
_____

POST NUMBER _____

POST DATE _____

NOTES _____
_____

POST

_____
_____
_____
_____

POST NUMBER _____

POST DATE _____

NOTES _____
_____

TWITTER POSTS *PLANNER*

POST

_____
_____
_____
_____

POST NUMBER _____

POST DATE _____

NOTES _____
_____

POST

_____
_____
_____
_____

POST NUMBER _____

POST DATE _____

NOTES _____
_____

POST

_____
_____
_____
_____

POST NUMBER _____

POST DATE _____

NOTES _____
_____

TWITTER POSTS *PLANNER*

POST

POST NUMBER _____

POST DATE _____

NOTES _____

_____

POST

POST NUMBER _____

POST DATE _____

NOTES _____

_____

POST

POST NUMBER _____

POST DATE _____

NOTES _____

_____

TWITTER POSTS *PLANNER*

POST

_____
_____
_____
_____

POST NUMBER _____

POST DATE _____

NOTES _____
_____

POST

_____
_____
_____
_____
_____

POST NUMBER _____

POST DATE _____

NOTES _____
_____

POST

_____
_____
_____
_____

POST NUMBER _____

POST DATE _____

NOTES _____
_____

TWITTER POSTS *PLANNER*

POST

_____
_____
_____
_____
_____

POST NUMBER _____

POST DATE _____

NOTES _____
_____

POST

_____
_____
_____
_____
_____

POST NUMBER _____

POST DATE _____

NOTES _____
_____

POST

_____
_____
_____
_____

POST NUMBER _____

POST DATE _____

NOTES _____
_____

TWITTER POSTS *PLANNER*

POST

_____
_____
_____
_____
_____

POST NUMBER _____

POST DATE _____

NOTES _____
_____

POST

_____
_____
_____
_____
_____

POST NUMBER _____

POST DATE _____

NOTES _____
_____

POST

_____
_____
_____
_____

POST NUMBER _____

POST DATE _____

NOTES _____
_____

TWITTER POSTS *PLANNER*

POST

_____
_____
_____
_____

POST NUMBER _____

POST DATE _____

NOTES _____
_____

POST

_____
_____
_____
_____

POST NUMBER _____

POST DATE _____

NOTES _____
_____

POST

_____
_____
_____
_____

POST NUMBER _____

POST DATE _____

NOTES _____
_____

TWITTER POSTS *PLANNER*

POST

POST NUMBER _____

POST DATE _____

NOTES _____
_____

POST

POST NUMBER _____

POST DATE _____

NOTES _____
_____

POST

POST NUMBER _____

POST DATE _____

NOTES _____
_____

TWITTER POSTS *PLANNER*

POST

_____
_____
_____
_____

POST NUMBER _____

POST DATE _____

NOTES _____
_____

POST

_____
_____
_____
_____

POST NUMBER _____

POST DATE _____

NOTES _____
_____

POST

_____
_____
_____
_____

POST NUMBER _____

POST DATE _____

NOTES _____
_____

TWITTER POSTS *PLANNER*

POST

_____
_____
_____
_____
_____

POST NUMBER _____

POST DATE _____

NOTES _____
_____

POST

_____
_____
_____
_____
_____

POST NUMBER _____

POST DATE _____

NOTES _____
_____

POST

_____
_____
_____
_____
_____

POST NUMBER _____

POST DATE _____

NOTES _____
_____

TWITTER POSTS *PLANNER*

POST

_____
_____
_____
_____

POST NUMBER _____

POST DATE _____

NOTES _____
_____

POST

_____
_____
_____
_____

POST NUMBER _____

POST DATE _____

NOTES _____
_____

POST

_____
_____
_____
_____

POST NUMBER _____

POST DATE _____

NOTES _____
_____

TWITTER POSTS *PLANNER*

POST

_____

_____

_____

_____

| POST NUMBER _____ |
| POST DATE _____ |
| NOTES _____ _____ |

POST

_____

_____

_____

_____

| POST NUMBER _____ |
| POST DATE _____ |
| NOTES _____ _____ |

POST

_____

_____

_____

_____

| POST NUMBER _____ |
| POST DATE _____ |
| NOTES _____ _____ |

TWITTER POSTS *PLANNER*

POST

_____

_____

_____

_____

_____

POST NUMBER _____

POST DATE _____

NOTES _____

_____

POST

_____

_____

_____

_____

_____

POST NUMBER _____

POST DATE _____

NOTES _____

_____

POST

_____

_____

_____

_____

_____

POST NUMBER _____

POST DATE _____

NOTES _____

_____

TWITTER POSTS *PLANNER*

POST

POST NUMBER _____

POST DATE _____

NOTES _____
_____

POST

POST NUMBER _____

POST DATE _____

NOTES _____
_____

POST

POST NUMBER _____

POST DATE _____

NOTES _____
_____

TWITTER POSTS *PLANNER*

POST

POST NUMBER _____

POST DATE _____

NOTES _____
_____

POST

POST NUMBER _____

POST DATE _____

NOTES _____
_____

POST

POST NUMBER _____

POST DATE _____

NOTES _____
_____

TWITTER POSTS *PLANNER*

(POST)

_____
_____
_____
_____
_____

POST NUMBER _____

POST DATE _____

NOTES _____
_____

(POST)

_____
_____
_____
_____
_____

POST NUMBER _____

POST DATE _____

NOTES _____
_____

(POST)

_____
_____
_____
_____
_____

POST NUMBER _____

POST DATE _____

NOTES _____
_____

TWITTER POSTS *PLANNER*

(POST)

_____
_____
_____
_____

POST NUMBER _____

POST DATE _____

NOTES _____
_____

(POST)

_____
_____
_____
_____

POST NUMBER _____

POST DATE _____

NOTES _____
_____

(POST)

_____
_____
_____
_____

POST NUMBER _____

POST DATE _____

NOTES _____
_____

TWITTER POSTS *PLANNER*

POST

_____

_____

_____

_____

_____

| POST NUMBER _____ |
| POST DATE _____ |
| NOTES _____
 _____ |

POST

_____

_____

_____

_____

_____

| POST NUMBER _____ |
| POST DATE _____ |
| NOTES _____
 _____ |

POST

_____

_____

_____

_____

_____

| POST NUMBER _____ |
| POST DATE _____ |
| NOTES _____
 _____ |

TWITTER POSTS *PLANNER*

POST

_____

_____

_____

_____

POST NUMBER _____

POST DATE _____

NOTES _____

_____

POST

_____

_____

_____

_____

POST NUMBER _____

POST DATE _____

NOTES _____

_____

POST

_____

_____

_____

_____

POST NUMBER _____

POST DATE _____

NOTES _____

_____

TWITTER POSTS *PLANNER*

POST

_____
_____
_____
_____

POST NUMBER _____

POST DATE _____

NOTES _____
_____

POST

_____
_____
_____
_____

POST NUMBER _____

POST DATE _____

NOTES _____
_____

POST

_____
_____
_____
_____

POST NUMBER _____

POST DATE _____

NOTES _____
_____

TWITTER POSTS *PLANNER*

POST

POST NUMBER _____

POST DATE _____

NOTES _____
_____

POST

POST NUMBER _____

POST DATE _____

NOTES _____
_____

POST

POST NUMBER _____

POST DATE _____

NOTES _____
_____

TWITTER POSTS *PLANNER*

POST

_____
_____
_____
_____

POST NUMBER _____

POST DATE _____

NOTES _____
_____

POST

_____
_____
_____
_____

POST NUMBER _____

POST DATE _____

NOTES _____
_____

POST

_____
_____
_____
_____

POST NUMBER _____

POST DATE _____

NOTES _____
_____

TWITTER POSTS *PLANNER*

(POST)

_____
_____
_____
_____

POST NUMBER _____

POST DATE _____

NOTES _____
_____

(POST)

_____
_____
_____
_____

POST NUMBER _____

POST DATE _____

NOTES _____
_____

(POST)

_____
_____
_____
_____

POST NUMBER _____

POST DATE _____

NOTES _____
_____

TWITTER POSTS *PLANNER*

POST

_____
_____
_____
_____
_____

POST NUMBER _____

POST DATE _____

NOTES _____
_____

POST

_____
_____
_____
_____
_____

POST NUMBER _____

POST DATE _____

NOTES _____
_____

POST

_____
_____
_____
_____
_____

POST NUMBER _____

POST DATE _____

NOTES _____
_____

TWITTER POSTS *PLANNER*

POST

POST NUMBER _____

POST DATE _____

NOTES _____
_____

POST

POST NUMBER _____

POST DATE _____

NOTES _____
_____

POST

POST NUMBER _____

POST DATE _____

NOTES _____
_____

TWITTER POSTS *PLANNER*

POST

_____
_____
_____
_____
_____

POST NUMBER _____

POST DATE _____

NOTES _____
_____

POST

_____
_____
_____
_____
_____

POST NUMBER _____

POST DATE _____

NOTES _____
_____

POST

_____
_____
_____
_____

POST NUMBER _____

POST DATE _____

NOTES _____
_____

TWITTER POSTS *PLANNER*

(POST)

POST NUMBER _____

POST DATE _____

NOTES _____

_____

(POST)

POST NUMBER _____

POST DATE _____

NOTES _____

_____

(POST)

POST NUMBER _____

POST DATE _____

NOTES _____

_____

TWITTER POSTS *PLANNER*

POST

_____
_____
_____
_____
_____

POST NUMBER _____

POST DATE _____

NOTES _____
_____

POST

_____
_____
_____
_____
_____

POST NUMBER _____

POST DATE _____

NOTES _____
_____

POST

_____
_____
_____
_____
_____

POST NUMBER _____

POST DATE _____

NOTES _____
_____

TWITTER POSTS *PLANNER*

(POST)

_____

POST NUMBER _____

POST DATE _____

NOTES _____

_____

(POST)

_____

POST NUMBER _____

POST DATE _____

NOTES _____

_____

(POST)

_____

POST NUMBER _____

POST DATE _____

NOTES _____

_____

TWITTER POSTS *PLANNER*

(POST)

_____
_____
_____
_____
_____

POST NUMBER _____

POST DATE _____

NOTES _____
_____

(POST)

_____
_____
_____
_____

POST NUMBER _____

POST DATE _____

NOTES _____
_____

(POST)

_____
_____
_____
_____

POST NUMBER _____

POST DATE _____

NOTES _____
_____

TWITTER POSTS *PLANNER*

POST

_____
_____
_____
_____

POST NUMBER _____

POST DATE _____

NOTES _____
_____

POST

_____
_____
_____
_____

POST NUMBER _____

POST DATE _____

NOTES _____
_____

POST

_____
_____
_____
_____

POST NUMBER _____

POST DATE _____

NOTES _____
_____

TWITTER POSTS *PLANNER*

POST

_____
_____
_____
_____

POST NUMBER _____

POST DATE _____

NOTES _____
_____

POST

_____
_____
_____
_____

POST NUMBER _____

POST DATE _____

NOTES _____
_____

POST

_____
_____
_____
_____

POST NUMBER _____

POST DATE _____

NOTES _____
_____

TWITTER POSTS *PLANNER*

POST

POST NUMBER _____

POST DATE _____

NOTES _____
_____

POST

POST NUMBER _____

POST DATE _____

NOTES _____
_____

POST

POST NUMBER _____

POST DATE _____

NOTES _____
_____

TWITTER POSTS *PLANNER*

(POST)

_____
_____
_____
_____
_____

POST NUMBER _____

POST DATE _____

NOTES _____
_____

(POST)

_____
_____
_____
_____
_____

POST NUMBER _____

POST DATF _____

NOTES _____
_____

(POST)

_____
_____
_____
_____
_____

POST NUMBER _____

POST DATE _____

NOTES _____
_____

TWITTER POSTS *PLANNER*

POST

POST NUMBER _____

POST DATE _____

NOTES _____

_____

POST

POST NUMBER _____

POST DATE _____

NOTES _____

_____

POST

POST NUMBER _____

POST DATE _____

NOTES _____

_____

TWITTER POSTS *PLANNER*

POST

_____

_____

_____

_____

POST NUMBER _____

POST DATE _____

NOTES _____

_____

POST

_____

_____

_____

_____

POST NUMBER _____

POST DATE _____

NOTES _____

_____

POST

_____

_____

_____

_____

POST NUMBER _____

POST DATE _____

NOTES _____

_____

TWITTER POSTS *PLANNER*

POST

_____
_____
_____
_____
_____

POST NUMBER _____

POST DATE _____

NOTES _____
_____

POST

_____
_____
_____
_____
_____

POST NUMBER _____

POST DATE _____

NOTES _____
_____

POST

_____
_____
_____
_____
_____

POST NUMBER _____

POST DATE _____

NOTES _____
_____

TWITTER POSTS *PLANNER*

POST

_____
_____
_____
_____

POST NUMBER _____

POST DATE _____

NOTES _____
_____

POST

_____
_____
_____
_____

POST NUMBER _____

POST DATE _____

NOTES _____
_____

POST

_____
_____
_____
_____

POST NUMBER _____

POST DATE _____

NOTES _____
_____

TWITTER POSTS *PLANNER*

POST

POST NUMBER _____

POST DATE _____

NOTES _____
_____

POST

POST NUMBER _____

POST DATE _____

NOTES _____
_____

POST

POST NUMBER _____

POST DATE _____

NOTES _____
_____

TWITTER POSTS *PLANNER*

POST
_____
_____
_____
_____
_____

POST NUMBER _____

POST DATE _____

NOTES _____
_____

POST
_____
_____
_____
_____
_____

POST NUMBER _____

POST DATE _____

NOTES _____
_____

POST
_____
_____
_____
_____
_____

POST NUMBER _____

POST DATE _____

NOTES _____
_____

TWITTER POSTS *PLANNER*

POST

_____
_____
_____
_____

POST NUMBER _____

POST DATE _____

NOTES _____
_____

POST

_____
_____
_____
_____

POST NUMBER _____

POST DATE _____

NOTES _____
_____

POST

_____
_____
_____
_____

POST NUMBER _____

POST DATE _____

NOTES _____
_____

TWITTER POSTS *PLANNER*

(POST)
_____
_____
_____
_____

POST NUMBER _____

POST DATE _____

NOTES _____
_____

(POST)
_____
_____
_____
_____

POST NUMBER _____

POST DATE _____

NOTES _____
_____

(POST)
_____
_____
_____
_____

POST NUMBER _____

POST DATE _____

NOTES _____
_____

TWITTER POSTS *PLANNER*

POST

POST NUMBER _____

POST DATE _____

NOTES _____
_____

POST

POST NUMBER _____

POST DATE _____

NOTES _____
_____

POST

POST NUMBER _____

POST DATE _____

NOTES _____
_____

TWITTER POSTS *PLANNER*

POST

POST NUMBER _____

POST DATE _____

NOTES _____
_____

POST

POST NUMBER _____

POST DATE _____

NOTES _____
_____

POST

POST NUMBER _____

POST DATE _____

NOTES _____
_____

TWITTER POSTS *PLANNER*

POST

_____

_____

_____

_____

POST NUMBER _____

POST DATE _____

NOTES _____

_____

POST

_____

_____

_____

_____

POST NUMBER _____

POST DATE _____

NOTES _____

_____

POST

_____

_____

_____

_____

POST NUMBER _____

POST DATE _____

NOTES _____

_____

TWITTER POSTS *PLANNER*

(POST)

_____
_____
_____
_____
_____

POST NUMBER _____

POST DATE _____

NOTES _____
_____

(POST)

_____
_____
_____
_____
_____

POST NUMBER _____

POST DATE _____

NOTES _____
_____

(POST)

_____
_____
_____
_____
_____

POST NUMBER _____

POST DATE _____

NOTES _____
_____

TWITTER POSTS *PLANNER*

POST

POST NUMBER _____

POST DATE _____

NOTES _____

POST

POST NUMBER _____

POST DATE _____

NOTES _____

POST

POST NUMBER _____

POST DATE _____

NOTES _____

TWITTER POSTS *PLANNER*

POST

_____
_____
_____
_____
_____

POST NUMBER _____

POST DATE _____

NOTES _____
_____

POST

_____
_____
_____
_____
_____

POST NUMBER _____

POST DATE _____

NOTES _____
_____

POST

_____
_____
_____
_____
_____

POST NUMBER _____

POST DATE _____

NOTES _____
_____

TWITTER POSTS *PLANNER*

POST

_____
_____
_____
_____

POST NUMBER _____

POST DATE _____

NOTES _____
_____

POST

_____
_____
_____
_____

POST NUMBER _____

POST DATE _____

NOTES _____
_____

POST

_____
_____
_____
_____

POST NUMBER _____

POST DATE _____

NOTES _____
_____

TWITTER POSTS *PLANNER*

POST

_____
_____
_____
_____

POST NUMBER _____

POST DATE _____

NOTES _____
_____

POST

_____
_____
_____
_____

POST NUMBER _____

POST DATE _____

NOTES _____
_____

POST

_____
_____
_____
_____

POST NUMBER _____

POST DATE _____

NOTES _____
_____

TWITTER POSTS *PLANNER*

POST

_____

POST NUMBER _____

POST DATE _____

NOTES _____
_____

POST

_____

POST NUMBER _____

POST DATE _____

NOTES _____
_____

POST

_____

POST NUMBER _____

POST DATE _____

NOTES _____
_____

TWITTER POSTS *PLANNER*

POST

_____
_____
_____
_____
_____

POST NUMBER _____

POST DATE _____

NOTES _____
_____

POST

_____
_____
_____
_____
_____

POST NUMBER _____

POST DATE _____

NOTES _____
_____

POST

_____
_____
_____
_____

POST NUMBER _____

POST DATE _____

NOTES _____
_____

TWITTER POSTS *PLANNER*

POST

_____
_____
_____
_____

POST NUMBER _____

POST DATE _____

NOTES _____
_____

POST

_____
_____
_____
_____

POST NUMBER _____

POST DATE _____

NOTES _____
_____

POST

_____
_____
_____
_____

POST NUMBER _____

POST DATE _____

NOTES _____
_____

TWITTER POSTS *PLANNER*

POST

_____
_____
_____
_____

POST NUMBER _____

POST DATE _____

NOTES _____
_____

POST

_____
_____
_____
_____

POST NUMBER _____

POST DATE _____

NOTES _____
_____

POST

_____
_____
_____
_____

POST NUMBER _____

POST DATE _____

NOTES _____
_____

TWITTER POSTS *PLANNER*

POST

POST NUMBER _____

POST DATE _____

NOTES _____

_____

POST

POST NUMBER _____

POST DATE _____

NOTES _____

_____

POST

POST NUMBER _____

POST DATE _____

NOTES _____

_____

TWITTER POSTS *PLANNER*

POST

_____

_____

_____

_____

_____

POST NUMBER _____

POST DATE _____

NOTES _____

_____

POST

_____

_____

_____

_____

_____

POST NUMBER _____

POST DATE _____

NOTES _____

_____

POST

_____

_____

_____

_____

_____

POST NUMBER _____

POST DATE _____

NOTES _____

_____

TWITTER POSTS *PLANNER*

POST

_____
_____
_____
_____
_____

POST NUMBER _____

POST DATE _____

NOTES _____
_____

POST

_____
_____
_____
_____
_____

POST NUMBER _____

POST DATE _____

NOTES _____
_____

POST

_____
_____
_____
_____
_____

POST NUMBER _____

POST DATE _____

NOTES _____
_____

TWITTER POSTS *PLANNER*

POST

_____

_____

_____

_____

_____

POST NUMBER _____

POST DATE _____

NOTES _____

_____

POST

_____

_____

_____

_____

_____

POST NUMBER _____

POST DATE _____

NOTES _____

_____

POST

_____

_____

_____

_____

_____

POST NUMBER _____

POST DATE _____

NOTES _____

_____

TWITTER POSTS *PLANNER*

POST

_____
_____
_____
_____
_____

POST NUMBER _____

POST DATE _____

NOTES _____
_____

POST

_____
_____
_____
_____
_____

POST NUMBER _____

POST DATE _____

NOTES _____
_____

POST

_____
_____
_____
_____
_____

POST NUMBER _____

POST DATE _____

NOTES _____
_____

TWITTER POSTS *PLANNER*

(POST)

_____
_____
_____
_____
_____

POST NUMBER _____

POST DATE _____

NOTES _____
_____

(POST)

_____
_____
_____
_____
_____

POST NUMBER _____

POST DATE _____

NOTES _____
_____

(POST)

_____
_____
_____
_____
_____

POST NUMBER _____

POST DATE _____

NOTES _____
_____

TWITTER POSTS *PLANNER*

POST

_____
_____
_____
_____
_____

POST NUMBER _____

POST DATE _____

NOTES _____
_____

POST

_____
_____
_____
_____
_____

POST NUMBER _____

POST DATE _____

NOTES _____
_____

POST

_____
_____
_____
_____
_____

POST NUMBER _____

POST DATE _____

NOTES _____
_____

TWITTER POSTS *PLANNER*

POST

_____
_____
_____
_____

POST NUMBER _____

POST DATE _____

NOTES _____
_____

POST

_____
_____
_____
_____
_____

POST NUMBER _____

POST DATE _____

NOTES _____
_____

POST

_____
_____
_____
_____

POST NUMBER _____

POST DATE _____

NOTES _____
_____

TWITTER POSTS *PLANNER*

POST

_____
_____
_____
_____

POST NUMBER _____

POST DATE _____

NOTES _____
_____

POST

_____
_____
_____
_____

POST NUMBER _____

POST DATE _____

NOTES _____
_____

POST

_____
_____
_____
_____

POST NUMBER _____

POST DATE _____

NOTES _____
_____

TWITTER POSTS *PLANNER*

POST

_____
_____
_____
_____

POST NUMBER _____

POST DATE _____

NOTES _____
_____

POST

_____
_____
_____
_____

POST NUMBER _____

POST DATF _____

NOTES _____
_____

POST

_____
_____
_____
_____

POST NUMBER _____

POST DATE _____

NOTES _____
_____

TWITTER POSTS *PLANNER*

POST

POST NUMBER _____

POST DATE _____

NOTES _____

POST

POST NUMBER _____

POST DATE _____

NOTES _____

POST

POST NUMBER _____

POST DATE _____

NOTES _____

TWITTER POSTS *PLANNER*

POST

_____
_____
_____
_____
_____

POST NUMBER _____

POST DATE _____

NOTES _____
_____

POST

_____
_____
_____
_____
_____

POST NUMBER _____

POST DATE _____

NOTES _____
_____

POST

_____
_____
_____
_____
_____

POST NUMBER _____

POST DATE _____

NOTES _____
_____

TWITTER POSTS *PLANNER*

(POST) _____

_____

_____

_____

_____

| POST NUMBER _____ |

| POST DATE _____ |

| NOTES _____ |
| _____ |

(POST) _____

_____

_____

_____

_____

| POST NUMBER _____ |

| POST DATE _____ |

| NOTES _____ |
| _____ |

(POST) _____

_____

_____

_____

_____

| POST NUMBER _____ |

| POST DATE _____ |

| NOTES _____ |
| _____ |

TWITTER POSTS *PLANNER*

POST

_____
_____
_____
_____
_____

POST NUMBER _____

POST DATE _____

NOTES _____
_____

POST

_____
_____
_____
_____
_____

POST NUMBER _____

POST DATE _____

NOTES _____
_____

POST

_____
_____
_____
_____
_____

POST NUMBER _____

POST DATE _____

NOTES _____
_____

TWITTER POSTS *PLANNER*

POST

_____
_____
_____
_____
_____

POST NUMBER _____

POST DATE _____

NOTES _____
_____

POST

_____
_____
_____
_____
_____

POST NUMBER _____

POST DATE _____

NOTES _____
_____

POST

_____
_____
_____
_____
_____

POST NUMBER _____

POST DATE _____

NOTES _____
_____

TWITTER POSTS *PLANNER*

POST

POST NUMBER _____

POST DATE _____

NOTES _____
_____

POST

POST NUMBER _____

POST DATF _____

NOTES _____
_____

POST

POST NUMBER _____

POST DATE _____

NOTES _____
_____

TWITTER POSTS *PLANNER*

POST

_____
_____
_____
_____
_____

POST NUMBER _____

POST DATE _____

NOTES _____
_____

POST

_____
_____
_____
_____
_____

POST NUMBER _____

POST DATE _____

NOTES _____
_____

POST

_____
_____
_____
_____
_____

POST NUMBER _____

POST DATE _____

NOTES _____
_____

TWITTER POSTS *PLANNER*

POST

_____
_____
_____
_____
_____

POST NUMBER _____

POST DATE _____

NOTES _____
_____

POST

_____
_____
_____
_____
_____

POST NUMBER _____

POST DATE _____

NOTES _____
_____

POST

_____
_____
_____
_____
_____

POST NUMBER _____

POST DATE _____

NOTES _____
_____

TWITTER POSTS *PLANNER*

POST

_____
_____
_____
_____
_____

POST NUMBER _____

POST DATE _____

NOTES _____
_____

POST

_____
_____
_____
_____
_____

POST NUMBER _____

POST DATE _____

NOTES _____
_____

POST

_____
_____
_____
_____
_____

POST NUMBER _____

POST DATE _____

NOTES _____
_____

TWITTER POSTS *PLANNER*

POST

_____
_____
_____
_____
_____

POST NUMBER _____

POST DATE _____

NOTES _____
_____

POST

_____
_____
_____
_____
_____

POST NUMBER _____

POST DATE _____

NOTES _____
_____

POST

_____
_____
_____
_____
_____

POST NUMBER _____

POST DATE _____

NOTES _____
_____

TWITTER POSTS *PLANNER*

(POST)

_____
_____
_____
_____
_____

POST NUMBER _____

POST DATE _____

NOTES _____
_____

(POST)

_____
_____
_____
_____
_____

POST NUMBER _____

POST DATE _____

NOTES _____
_____

(POST)

_____
_____
_____
_____
_____

POST NUMBER _____

POST DATE _____

NOTES _____
_____

TWITTER POSTS *PLANNER*

(POST)

POST NUMBER _____

POST DATE _____

NOTES _____
_____

(POST)

POST NUMBER _____

POST DATE _____

NOTES _____
_____

(POST)

POST NUMBER _____

POST DATE _____

NOTES _____
_____

TWITTER POSTS *PLANNER*

POST

POST NUMBER _____

POST DATE _____

NOTES _____
_____

POST

POST NUMBER _____

POST DATE _____

NOTES _____
_____

POST

POST NUMBER _____

POST DATE _____

NOTES _____
_____

TWITTER POSTS *PLANNER*

POST

_____
_____
_____
_____
_____

POST NUMBER _____

POST DATE _____

NOTES _____
_____

POST

_____
_____
_____
_____

POST NUMBER _____

POST DATE _____

NOTES _____
_____

POST

_____
_____
_____
_____

POST NUMBER _____

POST DATE _____

NOTES _____
_____

TWITTER POSTS *PLANNER*

POST

_____
_____
_____
_____

POST NUMBER _____

POST DATE _____

NOTES _____
_____

POST

_____
_____
_____
_____

POST NUMBER _____

POST DATE _____

NOTES _____
_____

POST

_____
_____
_____
_____

POST NUMBER _____

POST DATE _____

NOTES _____
_____

TWITTER POSTS *PLANNER*

(POST)

_____
_____
_____
_____
_____

POST NUMBER _____

POST DATE _____

NOTES _____
_____

(POST)

_____
_____
_____
_____
_____

POST NUMBER _____

POST DATE _____

NOTES _____
_____

(POST)

_____
_____
_____
_____
_____

POST NUMBER _____

POST DATE _____

NOTES _____
_____

TWITTER POSTS *PLANNER*

POST

_____

_____

_____

_____

_____

POST NUMBER _____

POST DATE _____

NOTES _____

_____

POST

_____

_____

_____

_____

_____

POST NUMBER _____

POST DATE _____

NOTES _____

_____

POST

_____

_____

_____

_____

POST NUMBER _____

POST DATE _____

NOTES _____

_____

TWITTER POSTS *PLANNER*

POST

_____
_____
_____
_____
_____

POST NUMBER _____

POST DATE _____

NOTES _____
_____

POST

_____
_____
_____
_____
_____

POST NUMBER _____

POST DATE _____

NOTES _____
_____

POST

_____
_____
_____
_____

POST NUMBER _____

POST DATE _____

NOTES _____
_____

TWITTER POSTS *PLANNER*

POST

POST NUMBER _____

POST DATE _____

NOTES _____

POST

POST NUMBER _____

POST DATE _____

NOTES _____

POST

POST NUMBER _____

POST DATE _____

NOTES _____

TWITTER POSTS *PLANNER*

POST

_____
_____
_____
_____
_____

POST NUMBER _____

POST DATE _____

NOTES _____
_____

POST

_____
_____
_____
_____

POST NUMBER _____

POST DATE _____

NOTES _____
_____

POST

_____
_____
_____
_____

POST NUMBER _____

POST DATE _____

NOTES _____
_____

TWITTER POSTS *PLANNER*

POST

_____
_____
_____
_____
_____

POST NUMBER _____

POST DATE _____

NOTES _____
_____

POST

_____
_____
_____
_____
_____

POST NUMBER _____

POST DATE _____

NOTES _____
_____

POST

_____
_____
_____
_____
_____

POST NUMBER _____

POST DATE _____

NOTES _____
_____

TWITTER POSTS *PLANNER*

POST

_____
_____
_____
_____

POST NUMBER _____

POST DATE _____

NOTES _____
_____

POST

_____
_____
_____
_____

POST NUMBER _____

POST DATE _____

NOTES _____
_____

POST

_____
_____
_____
_____

POST NUMBER _____

POST DATE _____

NOTES _____
_____

TWITTER POSTS *PLANNER*

POST

_____
_____
_____
_____
_____

POST NUMBER _____

POST DATE _____

NOTES _____
_____

POST

_____
_____
_____
_____
_____

POST NUMBER _____

POST DATE _____

NOTES _____
_____

POST

_____
_____
_____
_____
_____

POST NUMBER _____

POST DATE _____

NOTES _____
_____

TWITTER POSTS *PLANNER*

POST

_____
_____
_____
_____

POST NUMBER _____

POST DATE _____

NOTES _____
_____

POST

_____
_____
_____
_____

POST NUMBER _____

POST DATE _____

NOTES _____
_____

POST

_____
_____
_____
_____

POST NUMBER _____

POST DATE _____

NOTES _____
_____

TWITTER POSTS *PLANNER*

(POST)

_____
_____
_____
_____
_____

POST NUMBER _____

POST DATE _____

NOTES _____
_____

(POST)

_____
_____
_____
_____
_____

POST NUMBER _____

POST DATE _____

NOTES _____
_____

(POST)

_____
_____
_____
_____
_____

POST NUMBER _____

POST DATE _____

NOTES _____
_____

TWITTER POSTS *PLANNER*

(POST) _____

_____

_____

_____

_____

POST NUMBER _____

POST DATE _____

NOTES _____

_____

(POST) _____

_____

_____

_____

_____

POST NUMBER _____

POST DATE _____

NOTES _____

_____

(POST) _____

_____

_____

_____

_____

POST NUMBER _____

POST DATE _____

NOTES _____

_____

TWITTER POSTS *PLANNER*

POST

_____
_____
_____
_____
_____

POST NUMBER _____

POST DATE _____

NOTES _____
_____

POST

_____
_____
_____
_____
_____

POST NUMBER _____

POST DATE _____

NOTES _____
_____

POST

_____
_____
_____
_____
_____

POST NUMBER _____

POST DATE _____

NOTES _____
_____

TWITTER POSTS *PLANNER*

(POST)

POST NUMBER _____

POST DATE _____

NOTES _____

(POST)

POST NUMBER _____

POST DATE _____

NOTES _____

(POST)

POST NUMBER _____

POST DATE _____

NOTES _____

TWITTER POSTS *PLANNER*

POST

POST NUMBER _____

POST DATE _____

NOTES _____

POST

POST NUMBER _____

POST DATE _____

NOTES _____

POST

POST NUMBER _____

POST DATE _____

NOTES _____

TWITTER POSTS *PLANNER*

(POST)

_____
_____
_____
_____
_____

POST NUMBER _____

POST DATE _____

NOTES _____
_____

(POST)

_____
_____
_____
_____
_____

POST NUMBER _____

POST DATE _____

NOTES _____
_____

(POST)

_____
_____
_____
_____
_____

POST NUMBER _____

POST DATE _____

NOTES _____
_____

TWITTER POSTS *PLANNER*

POST

POST NUMBER _____

POST DATE _____

NOTES _____
_____

POST

POST NUMBER _____

POST DATE _____

NOTES _____
_____

POST

POST NUMBER _____

POST DATE _____

NOTES _____
_____

TWITTER POSTS *PLANNER*

POST

_____

_____

_____

_____

_____

POST NUMBER _____

POST DATE _____

NOTES _____

_____

POST

_____

_____

_____

_____

POST NUMBER _____

POST DATE _____

NOTES _____

_____

POST

_____

_____

_____

_____

POST NUMBER _____

POST DATE _____

NOTES _____

_____

TWITTER POSTS *PLANNER*

POST

_____
_____
_____
_____
_____

POST NUMBER _____

POST DATE _____

NOTES _____
_____

POST

_____
_____
_____
_____
_____

POST NUMBER _____

POST DATE _____

NOTES _____
_____

POST

_____
_____
_____
_____
_____

POST NUMBER _____

POST DATE _____

NOTES _____
_____

TWITTER POSTS *PLANNER*

POST

_____
_____
_____
_____
_____

POST NUMBER _____

POST DATE _____

NOTES _____
_____

POST

_____
_____
_____
_____
_____

POST NUMBER _____

POST DATE _____

NOTES _____
_____

POST

_____
_____
_____
_____
_____

POST NUMBER _____

POST DATE _____

NOTES _____
_____

TWITTER POSTS *PLANNER*

POST

_____
_____
_____
_____
_____

POST NUMBER _____

POST DATE _____

NOTES _____
_____

POST

_____
_____
_____
_____
_____

POST NUMBER _____

POST DATE _____

NOTES _____
_____

POST

_____
_____
_____
_____

POST NUMBER _____

POST DATE _____

NOTES _____
_____

TWITTER POSTS *PLANNER*

POST

_____
_____
_____
_____
_____

POST NUMBER _____

POST DATE _____

NOTES _____
_____

POST

_____
_____
_____
_____
_____

POST NUMBER _____

POST DATE _____

NOTES _____
_____

POST

_____
_____
_____
_____
_____

POST NUMBER _____

POST DATE _____

NOTES _____
_____

TWITTER POSTS *PLANNER*

POST

POST NUMBER _____

POST DATE _____

NOTES _____
_____

POST

POST NUMBER _____

POST DATE _____

NOTES _____
_____

POST

POST NUMBER _____

POST DATE _____

NOTES _____
_____

TWITTER POSTS *PLANNER*

POST

_____
_____
_____
_____

POST NUMBER _____

POST DATE _____

NOTES _____
_____

POST

_____
_____
_____
_____

POST NUMBER _____

POST DATE _____

NOTES _____
_____

POST

_____
_____
_____
_____

POST NUMBER _____

POST DATE _____

NOTES _____
_____

TWITTER POSTS *PLANNER*

POST

POST NUMBER _____

POST DATE _____

NOTES _____

_____

POST

POST NUMBER _____

POST DATE _____

NOTES _____

_____

POST

POST NUMBER _____

POST DATE _____

NOTES _____

_____

TWITTER POSTS *PLANNER*

POST

_____
_____
_____
_____
_____

POST NUMBER _____

POST DATE _____

NOTES _____
_____

POST

_____
_____
_____
_____
_____

POST NUMBER _____

POST DATE _____

NOTES _____
_____

POST

_____
_____
_____
_____
_____

POST NUMBER _____

POST DATE _____

NOTES _____
_____

TWITTER POSTS *PLANNER*

POST

POST NUMBER _____

POST DATE _____

NOTES _____

_____

POST

POST NUMBER _____

POST DATE _____

NOTES _____

_____

POST

POST NUMBER _____

POST DATE _____

NOTES _____

_____

TWITTER POSTS *PLANNER*

POST

_____
_____
_____
_____

POST NUMBER _____

POST DATE _____

NOTES _____
_____

POST

_____
_____
_____
_____

POST NUMBER _____

POST DATE _____

NOTES _____
_____

POST

_____
_____
_____
_____

POST NUMBER _____

POST DATE _____

NOTES _____
_____

TWITTER POSTS *PLANNER*

POST

_____
_____
_____
_____

POST NUMBER _____

POST DATE _____

NOTES _____
_____

POST

_____
_____
_____
_____

POST NUMBER _____

POST DATE _____

NOTES _____
_____

POST

_____
_____
_____
_____

POST NUMBER _____

POST DATE _____

NOTES _____
_____

TWITTER POSTS *PLANNER*

POST

_____
_____
_____
_____
_____

POST NUMBER _____

POST DATE _____

NOTES _____
_____

POST

_____
_____
_____
_____
_____

POST NUMBER _____

POST DATE _____

NOTES _____
_____

POST

_____
_____
_____
_____

POST NUMBER _____

POST DATE _____

NOTES _____
_____

TWITTER POSTS *PLANNER*

POST

_____
_____
_____
_____
_____

POST NUMBER _____

POST DATE _____

NOTES _____
_____

POST

_____
_____
_____
_____
_____

POST NUMBER _____

POST DATE _____

NOTES _____
_____

POST

_____
_____
_____
_____

POST NUMBER _____

POST DATE _____

NOTES _____
_____

TWITTER POSTS *PLANNER*

POST

_____
_____
_____
_____
_____

POST NUMBER _____

POST DATE _____

NOTES _____
_____

POST

_____
_____
_____
_____
_____

POST NUMBER _____

POST DATE _____

NOTES _____
_____

POST

_____
_____
_____
_____
_____

POST NUMBER _____

POST DATE _____

NOTES _____
_____

TWITTER POSTS *PLANNER*

POST

POST NUMBER _____

POST DATE _____

NOTES _____

POST

POST NUMBER _____

POST DATE _____

NOTES _____

POST

POST NUMBER _____

POST DATE _____

NOTES _____

TWITTER POSTS *PLANNER*

(POST)

_____
_____
_____
_____
_____

POST NUMBER _____

POST DATE _____

NOTES _____
_____

(POST)

_____
_____
_____
_____
_____

POST NUMBER _____

POST DATE _____

NOTES _____
_____

(POST)

_____
_____
_____
_____
_____

POST NUMBER _____

POST DATE _____

NOTES _____
_____

CPSIA information can be obtained
at www.ICGtesting.com
Printed in the USA
BVHW051048150221
600147BV00011B/914